Penguin Chicks

Julie Murray

Abdo
BABY ANIMALS
Kids

abdopublishing.com

Published by Abdo Kids, a division of ABDO, PO Box 398166, Minneapolis, Minnesota 55439.
Copyright © 2018 by Abdo Consulting Group, Inc. International copyrights reserved in all countries.
No part of this book may be reproduced in any form without written permission from the publisher.

Printed in the United States of America, North Mankato, Minnesota.

052017

092017

THIS BOOK CONTAINS RECYCLED MATERIALS

Photo Credits: Glow Images, iStock, Shutterstock

Production Contributors: Teddy Borth, Jennie Forsberg, Grace Hansen

Design Contributors: Christina Doffing, Candice Keimig, Dorothy Toth

Publisher's Cataloging in Publication Data

Names: Murray, Julie, 1969-, author.

Title: Penguin chicks / by Julie Murray.

Description: Minneapolis, Minnesota : Abdo Kids, 2018 | Series: Baby animals |
    Includes bibliographical references and index.

Identifiers: LCCN 2016962296 | ISBN 9781532100055 (lib. bdg.) |
    ISBN 9781532100741 (ebook) | ISBN 9781532101298 (Read-to-me ebook)

Subjects: LCSH: Penguins--Juvenile literature. | Penguins--Infancy--Juvenile literature.

Classification: DDC 598.47--dc23

LC record available at http://lccn.loc.gov/2016962296

Table of Contents

Penguin Chicks

A baby penguin is a chick.

A penguin lays two eggs. They are kept warm until they **hatch**.

Crack! Crack! The chicks come out of the eggs.

They stay close to mom and dad. This keeps them safe and warm.

They have **fine** and fluffy feathers. They cannot swim yet.

Mom and dad feed them.

They like to eat krill and fish.

They live in a large group.

It is called a colony.

They grow thick feathers.

They are black and white.

Now they are ready to swim.

They have flippers. They also have **webbed** feet. They can swim fast!

Watch a Gentoo Penguin Grow!

newborn

45 days

4 months

3 years

Glossary

fine
thin and wispy.

hatch
to come from an egg.

thick
made up of a large number of things that are close together.

webbed
having toes connected by skin.

Index

abdokids.com

Use this code to log on to abdokids.com and access crafts, games, videos, and more!

Abdo Kids Code:
BPKO055